The Way of Life

according to Laotzu

Anonymous, twelfth century: A Branch of White Jasmine.

The

Way of Life

according to Laotzu

AN AMERICAN VERSION
BY WITTER BYNNER

A Perigee Book

Perigee Books
are published by
The Putnam Publishing Group
200 Madison Avenue
New York, NY 10016

Calligraphy by Li Ging Guay
Designed by Liney Li

ISBN 0-399-51298-5

To

Kiang Kang-hu

my collaborator for a decade (1918-1929) on
The Jade Mountain, who finally received a copy
of my *The Way of Life* in a Nanking prison in
1948 and wrote me before his death in 1954 in
a Shanghai prison this reassurance:

> . . . *It is impossible to translate it without an
> interpretation. Most of the translations were
> based on the interpretations of commentators,
> but you chiefly took its interpretation from
> your own insight. It was your "fore-nature"
> understanding—or in Chinese,* hsien-t'ien—
> *that rendered it so simple and yet so profound.
> So the translation could be very close to the
> original text even without knowledge of the
> words. I am rather shameful that I could not
> assist you in any way.*

"The way to do is to be."

LAOTZU

LEGENDS as to Laotzu are more or less familiar.

Immaculately conceived to a shooting-star, carried in his mother's womb for sixty-two years and born, it is said, white-haired, in 604 B.C., he became in due time keeper of imperial archives at Loyang, an ancient capital in what is now the Chinese province of Honan.

Speaking wisdom which attracted followers, he had refused to the end of his life to set it down: considering the way of life and the ways of the world, he had decided that a great deal was done and said in the world which might better be spared. His choice, however, was not, as has been widely assumed, vacant inaction or passive contemplation. It was creative quietism. Though he realized the fact that action can be emptier than inaction, he was no more than Walt Whitman a believer in abstention from deed. He knew that a man can be a doer without being an actor and by no means banned being of use when he said that "the way to do is to be." Twenty-five centuries before Whitman, he knew the value of loafing and inviting one's soul; and the American poet, whether or not consciously, has been in many ways one of the Chinese poet's more eminent Western disciples, as Thoreau has been also, with his tenet, "Be it life or death, we seek only reality." But Whitman and Thoreau loved written words, whereas Laotzu felt that written words by defining, by limiting, could have dubious effects. Aware of the dangers inherent in dogma, he was reluctant to leave a set record of his own spoken belief, lest it become to followers an outer and formal rather than an inner and natural faith, an outside authority rather than intuition. He laid down no rigid laws for behavior: men's conduct should depend on their instinct and conscience. His last wish would have been to create other men in his own image; but he gently continued in life, by example presumably and by spoken word, suggesting to his neighbors and his emperor how natural, easy and happy a condition it is for men to be members of one another.

How do I know this integrity?
Because it could all begin in me.

One who recognizes all men as members of his
    own body
Is a sound man to guard them.

Legendary or true, it is told that Confucius, impressed by Laotzu's influence on people, visited him once to ask advice, ironically enough, on points of ceremonial etiquette. Baffled by the answers of the older man, to whom etiquette meant hypocrisy and nonsense, Confucius returned to his disciples and told them: "Of

12

birds I know that they have wings to fly with, of fish that they have fins to swim with, of wild beasts that they have feet to run with. For feet there are traps, for fins nets, for wings arrows. But who knows how dragons surmount wind and cloud into heaven? This day I have seen Laotzu and he is a dragon."

The end of the life legend is that, saddened by men's tragic perversity, their indisposition to accept "the way of life," to use life with natural goodness, with serene and integral respect, Laotzu rode away alone on a water-buffalo into the desert beyond the boundary of civilization, the great wall of his period. It is narrated that when he arrived at one of its gates, a warden there, Yin Hsi, who had had a dream of the sage's coming, recognized him from the dream and persuaded him to forego his reluctance and to record the principles of his philosophy. The result is said to have been the *Tao Teh Ching*, tao meaning the way of all life, teh the fit use of life by men and ching a text or classic. And from the gate-house or from somewhere, this testament of man's fitness in the universe, this text of five thousand words, comprising eighty-one sayings, many of them in verse, has come down through the centuries.

In written history there is little basis for these legends. Record of the philosopher appears first—a brief account ending, "No one knows where he died"—in the annals of Ssu Ma Ch'ien, born five hundred years after Laotzu; and some Western scholars, like some of their Eastern predecessors, have believed that long-lived Laotzu was a myth and that the sayings attributed to him were a compilation of the sayings of a number of men who lived during the next two or three hundred years. Gowen and Hall in their *Outline History of China* say that the *Tao Teh Ching* "is very probably the work of a later age, perhaps of the second century B.C., but is generally regarded as containing many of the sayings of the sage." In an essay accompanying the Buddhist-minded translation by Wai-tao and Dwight Goddard, Dr. Kiang Kang-hu is more specific. "Three Taoist sages," he writes, "who lived two or three hundred or more years apart, according to history, are commonly believed to be the same man, who by his wisdom had attained longevity . . . The simpler and more probable solution of the confusion is to accept the historicity of all three but to give credit for the original writing to Laotzu and consider the others as able disciples and possibly editors. The book in its present form might not have been written until the third century B.C. . . . for it was engraved on stone tablets soon after that time." It might, he thinks, have contained verses by later Taoists "without detracting from the larger credit that belongs to Laotzu." The earliest known manuscript dates from the T'ang Dynasty, a thousand years later. In *A Criticism of Some Recent Methods of Dating Laotzu*, Dr. Hu Shih has shown that the methods of internal evidence used to impugn the authenticity of Laotzu's writings might have cast similar doubt on the writings of Confucius or of almost anyone. Mark Twain's comment that *Hamlet* was written by Shakespeare or by some one else of the same name is pertinent. The *Tao Teh*

Ching is a book, an important and coherent book; and its value comes not from the outward identity or identities but from the inward and homogeneous identity of whoever wrote it.

More relevant is a divergence of judgment as to the book's value. Herbert Giles, the able, pioneering British sinophile, tender toward Confucian orthodoxy and finding in Laotzu "direct antagonism to it," wrote in his *Chinese Literature* published at the turn of the century that "scant allusion would have been made" to the *Tao Teh Ching*, "were it not for the attention paid to it by several more or less eminent foreign students of the language."

Perhaps pedantic Giles was annoyed by the fact that Laotzu could speak of scholars as a corrupting nuisance. Other scholars more imaginative than Giles have differed with him; and current tendency gives the mystical ethics of Laotzu a surer place in import for the world than the practical proprieties of Confucius. Certainly *Tao* has had profound influence on a great part of the world's population. Apart from the superstitious and the misled who have taken over the name for religious sects and have perverted its meaning into alchemy, geomancy, occultism, church tricks generally, a majority in the Oriental world has been fundamentally informed by Taoist quietism, whether or not they realize the source of the patience, forbearance and fortitude which characterize them. Not only has Laotzu's creative quietism been the foundation of China's age-long survival; what was originally good in Japanese Shin*tao*ism has also de-

15

rived from him. And the Western world might well temper its characteristic faults by taking Laotzu to heart.

Herrymon Maurer in a postscript to *The Old Fellow*, his fictional portrait of Laotzu, notes how closely the use of life according to Laotzu relates to the principles of democracy. Maurer is right that democracy cannot be a successful general practice unless it is first a true individual conviction. Many of us in the West think ourselves believers in democracy if we can point to one of its fading flowers even while the root of it in our own lives is gone with worms. No one in history has shown better than Laotzu how to keep the root of democracy clean. Not only democracy but all of life, he points out, grows at one's own doorstep. Maurer says, "Laotzu is one of our chief weapons against tanks, artillery and bombs." I agree that no one has bettered the ancient advice:

"Conduct your triumph as a funeral."

"In this life," reflected Sarah, Duchess of Marlborough in an eighteenth-century letter to her granddaughter, "I am satisfied there is nothing to be done but to make the best of what cannot be helped, to act with reason oneself and with a good conscience. And though that will not give all the joys some people wish for, yet it will make one very quiet." Laotzu's quietism is nothing but the fundamental sense commonly inherent in mankind, a common-sense so profound in its simplicity that it has come to be called mysticism. Mysticism or not, it seems to me the straightest, most

16

logical explanation as yet advanced for the continuance of life, the most logical use yet advised for enjoying it. While most of us, as we use life, try to open the universe to ourselves, Laotzu opens himself to the universe. If the views of disciples or commentators have sifted into his text, the original intent and integrity shine through nonetheless. All the deadening paraphernalia wished on him by priests and scholars cannot hide him. He remains as freshly and as universally alive as childhood. Followers of most religions or philosophies, feeling called upon to follow beyond reason, follow only a little way. Laotzu's logical, practical suggestions are both reasonable and simple.

However, if metaphysical or scholarly terms seem necessary for understanding, Dr. I. W. Heysinger relates Laotzu's basic concept to that of Roames, Darwin's pupil and co-worker: "the integrating principle of the whole—the Spirit, as it were, of the universe—instinct with contrivance, which flows with purpose" and to the philosophy of Lamarck. I myself have found Socrates and Plato in it, Marcus Aurelius and Tolstoi. More modernly it is at the heart of Mrs. Eddy's doctrines or of Bergson's creative evolution. Many a contemporary cult would do well to stop fumbling at the edges of Tao, to forget its priests who invented the ouija board and to go to its center.

Concerned with this center, Dr. Lin Yutang says in *The Wisdom of India and China:* "If there is one book in the whole of Oriental literature which should be read above all the others, it is, in my opinion, Laotzu's *Book*

17

of Tao . . . It is one of the profoundest books in the world's philosophy . . . profound and clear, mystic and practical."

He says this in the preface to his own English version of *The Book of Tao.* I had hoped that this version would be enough clearer than others in English to explain for me the influence of Laotzu on many of the T'ang poets, with whom I had become acquainted through Dr. Kiang Kang-hu's literal texts. With all admiration for Dr. Lin's Chinese spirit and English prose, I found myself little better satisfied with his presentation of Laotzu in Western free verse than I have been with other English versions, most of which have seemed to me dry and stiff, pompous and obscure. And that is why I have been led to make my own version.

Though I cannot read Chinese, two years spent in China and eleven years of work with Dr. Kiang in translating *The Jade Mountain* have given me a fair sense of the "spirit of the Chinese people" and an assiduity in finding English equivalents for idiom which literal translation fails to convey. And now, through various and varying English versions of the *Tao Teh Ching,* I have probed for the meaning as I recognize it and have persistently sought for it the clearest and simplest English expression I could discover. Above all I have been prompted by hope to acquaint Western readers with the heart of a Chinese poet whose head has been too much studied.

I have used, incidentally, even when I quote in this preface from those who use other orthography, the

Shen Chou (1427-1509): Walking with a Staff.

spellings Laotzu and *Tao Teh Ching* as preferable for the English or American ear and eye. And perhaps I shall be taken to task for using two or three times an unorthodox interpretation of text. But might not Laotzu's expression, for example, to "stand below other people," usually translated to "humble oneself below them," have been an ancient origin of our own word, "to understand"?

"There can be little doubt," says Walter Gorn Old, "that any translation from the Chinese is capable of extreme flexibility and license, of which, indeed the translator must avail himself if he would rightly render the spirit rather than the letter of the text; and the spirit, after all, is the essential thing, if we follow the teaching of Laotzu. It is safe to say that the more literal the translation may be the more obscure its meaning." Some of the *Tao Teh Ching* sayings, I am told, jingle repetitively with a surface lightness like that of nursery rhymes; and I have now and then ventured such effects, besides using rhyme whenever it felt natural to the sense and stayed by the text. Dr. Heysinger, deft and honest though his version is, sometimes lets the exactions of prosody dilate and dilute his writing. Dr. Lin Yutang's faithfulness, on the other hand, like Arthur Waley's, stays by expressions significant to Eastern but not to Western readers; and Laotzu should, I am convinced, be brought close to people in their own idiom, as a being beyond race or age.

As to other translations, Walter Gorn Old's has been popular in England and its comparatively direct word-

21

ing is accompanied by brief friendly essays of both Buddhist and Christian tinge, Arthur Waley's is painstakingly accurate and scholarly but difficult for any but scholars to follow, and there are several which are overcolored with Buddhism. Despite some fourteen offerings, and despite the fact that "the wording of the original," according to Dr. Lionel Giles, keeper of Oriental manuscripts in the British Museum, "is extraordinarily vigorous and terse," Westerners have not yet, in my judgment, been given a sufficiently intelligible version of Laotzu. Now that East and West have met, I suspect that every coming generation of Westerners will, in its own turn, in its own preferred words, try to express Laotzu's conception of the way and use of life. Though he himself said that words cannot express existence, he himself trespassed into them for his own generation.

Together with this absence of a forthright and congenial English translation, there are two other principal reasons why Laotzu has not as yet endeared himself to many Westerners. As religion on the one hand, as philosophy on the other, Taoism has been adulterated and complicated by its Oriental adherents. "The Taoist religion," writes Dr. Kiang, "is an abuse of Taoist philosophy. We find nothing essentially in common between them and, in many respects, they are conflicting." He elaborates upon this abuse, as he might have done upon ecclesiastical abuse of the philosophy of Jesus; but he does not, in my Occidental judgment, sufficiently emphasize the disservice done Laotzu by academicians. As the master himself said of the sensible man he commended,

> The cultured might call him heathenish,
> This man of few words, because his one care
> Is not to interfere but to let nature restore
> The sense of direction most men ignore,

and as he said also,

> False teachers of the way of life use flowery words
> And start nonsense.

Even Laotzu's most famous disciple, Chuangtzu, playfully complicated his master's firm, calm teaching; and the do-nothing idea has been so stressed a misreading as to alienate or puzzle many a Westerner who, seeing Laotzu steadily and whole, would have understood him and responded. Quakers, for instance, would be better Quakers for knowing Tao. Not all Westerners are natural addicts of the strenuous life.

But finally Dr. Kiang is right. Worse than the disservice done the sensible master by some of his scholarly followers has been the wrong done him by the religionists who have preempted him.

Laotzu knew that organization and institution interfere with a man's responsibility to himself and therefore with his proper use of life, that the more any outside authority interferes with a man's use of life and the less the man uses it according to his own instinct and conscience, the worse for the man and the worse for society. The only authority is "the way of life" itself;

a man's sense of it is the only priest or prophet. And yet, as travelers have seen Taoism in China, it is a cult compounded of devils and derelicts, a priest-ridden clutter of superstitions founded on ignorance and fear. As an organized religion, its initial and main sect having been established in the first century A.D. by a Pope named Chang Tao-lin, Taoism has even less to do with its founder than most cults have to do with the founders from whom they profess derivation. Even in modern China a Taoist papacy is paid to exorcize demons out of rich homes. To symbolize the patches of a beggar's cloak in Buddhistic ritual, fine brocades are cut into squares and then pieced together again in aesthetically broken design; Christ's cross has been made the pattern for palatial temples; and Laotzu's faith in the naturally and openly beneficent flow of life has been distorted into a commanding but hidden breath of dragons, his simple delighted awareness of the way of life has been twisted into a quest for the philosopher's stone. Thus men love to turn the simplest and most human of their species into complex and superhuman beings; thus everywhere men yearn to be misled by magicians; thus priests and cults in all lands and under virtuous guise make of ethics a craft and a business.

Confucius had the wisdom to forbid that a religion be based on his personality or codes; and his injunction against graven images has fared better than a similar injunction in the Ten Commandments. Hence Confucius continues unchanged as a realistic philosopher, an early pragmatist, while Laotzu and Jesus, his ethical fellows, have been tampered with by prelates, have been more and more removed from human living and relegated as mystics to a supernatural world.

Confucius prescribed formalized rather than spontaneous conduct for the development of superior men in their relation not only to the structure of society but to themselves. Laotzu, with little liking for organized thought or recruited action, no final faith in any authority but the authority of the heart, suggests that if those in charge of human affairs would act on instinct and conscience there would be less and less need of organized authority for governing people or, at any rate —and here he is seen as the realist he remains, as a man aware of necessarily gradual steps—less need for "superior men" to show. In our own time we have had evidence of the tragic effects of showy authority. In this dislike of show, rather than in any fundament of ethics, lay most of what Giles considered Laotzu's "direct antagonism" to Confucian orthodoxy. The trouble was that Confucius so ritualized his ethical culture that conduct of life took on forms similar to those of religion, whereas Laotzu spurned both religious and civil ceremony as misleading and harmful spectacle, his faith and conduct depending upon no outward prop but upon inner accord with the conscience of the universe.

Faith of this sort is true mysticism. Yet nothing could be further from the realistic core of Laotzu's way of life than Wilder Hobson's description of it as "that great mystical doctrine which holds that by profound,

25

solitary meditation men may obtain knowledge of the Absolute."

Laotzu was concerned, as man must ever be, with the origin and meaning of life but knew and declared that no man's explanation of it is absolute. His book opens,

> Existence is beyond the power of words
> To define,
> Terms may be used
> But are none of them absolute.

In at all considering the origin of life he was a mystic, as anyone must be, theist or atheist, who ventures either positive or negative guess concerning what is beyond the mind of man to know; and insofar as Laotzu's sayings probe this region he differed again from Confucius who, contentedly agnostic, restricted his philosophy to known nature and empirical bound. Laotzu, on the other hand, fused mysticism and pragmatism into a philosophy as realistic as that of Confucius but sweetened by the natural and sufficient intuition of rightness with which he believed all men to be endowed and by which he believed all men could discover their lives to be peaceful, useful and happy. He was by no means the solitary, unneighborly hermit, occult with meditation. He was as natural, as genial, as homely as Lincoln. Having a sense of proportion, he had a sense of humor and, as much as any man who has lived, was the everlasting neighbor. At least this is my reading of him from the one record by which he may be appraised.

26

It is worthy of note, moreover, that his philosophy anticipated and contained the humanitarian philosophies which have succeeded it, conflicting with none of them, deepening them all. It is a fair guess that neither the great Indian nor the great Jew would have found anything unacceptable in Laotzu's mystical uses, which have been made no more mystical by the one, no more useful by the other. Connecting not only mystically but practically with the springs and ends of our action, our thought, our being, it is a fundamental expression of everything in the heart and mind of men which respects, enjoys and serves the individual good by respecting, enjoying and serving the common good.

Though without the help this time of Dr. Kiang, who is beyond reach in China, and though mindful of Arthur Waley's distinction between scriptural and historical translation, I wait no longer to offer my reading of a poet whom I trust other readers will find with me to be neither occult nor complex but open and simple, neither pontifical nor archaic but lay and current, in his calm human stature.

Witter Bynner

Chapala, Jalisco, Mexico,
June 15, 1944.

The Way of Life

according to Laotzu

I

Existence is beyond the power of words
To define:
Terms may be used
But are none of them absolute.
In the beginning of heaven and earth there were no
 words,
Words came out of the womb of matter;
And whether a man dispassionately
Sees to the core of life
Or passionately
Sees the surface,
The core and the surface
Are essentially the same,
Words making them seem different
Only to express appearance.
If name be needed, wonder names them both:
From wonder into wonder
Existence opens.

2

People through finding something beautiful
Think something else unbeautiful,
Through finding one man fit
Judge another unfit.
Life and death, though stemming from each other,
        seem to conflict as stages of change,
Difficult and easy as phases of achievement,
Long and short as measures of contrast,
High and low as degrees of relation;
But, since the varying of tones gives music to a voice
And what is is the was of what shall be,
The sanest man
Sets up no deed,
Lays down no law,
Takes everything that happens as it comes,
As something to animate, not to appropriate,
To earn, not to own,
To accept naturally without self-importance:
If you never assume importance
You never lose it.

3

It is better not to make merit a matter of reward
Lest people conspire and contend,
Not to pile up rich belongings
Lest they rob,

Not to excite by display
Lest they covet.
A sound leader's aim
Is to open people's hearts,
Fill their stomachs,
Calm their wills,
Brace their bones
And so to clarify their thoughts and cleanse their needs
That no cunning meddler could touch them:
Without being forced, without strain or constraint,
Good government comes of itself.

4

Existence, by nothing bred,
Breeds everything.
Parent of the universe,
It smooths rough edges,
Unties hard knots,
Tempers the sharp sun,
Lays blowing dust,
Its image in the wellspring never fails.
But how was it conceived?—this image
Of no other sire.

5

Nature, immune as to a sacrifice of straw dogs,
Faces the decay of its fruits.
A sound man, immune as to a sacrifice of straw dogs,
Faces the passing of human generations.
The universe, like a bellows,
Is always emptying, always full:
The more it yields, the more it holds.
Men come to their wit's end arguing about it
And had better meet it at the marrow.

6

The breath of life moves through a deathless valley
Of mysterious motherhood
Which conceives and bears the universal seed,
The seeming of a world never to end,
Breath for men to draw from as they will:
And the more they take of it, the more remains.

7

The universe is deathless,
Is deathless because, having no finite self,
It stays infinite.
A sound man by not advancing himself
Stays the further ahead of himself,
By not confining himself to himself
Sustains himself outside himself:
By never being an end in himself
He endlessly becomes himself.

8

Man at his best, like water,
Serves as he goes along:
Like water he seeks his own level,
The common level of life,
Loves living close to the earth,
Living clear down in his heart,
Loves kinship with his neighbors,
The pick of words that tell the truth,
The even tenor of a well-run state,
The fair profit of able dealing,
The right timing of useful deeds,
And for blocking no one's way
No one blames him.

9

Keep stretching a bow
You repent of the pull,
A whetted saw
Goes thin and dull,
Surrounded with treasure
You lie ill at ease,
Proud beyond measure
You come to your knees:
Do enough, without vieing,
Be living, not dying.

10

Can you hold the door of your tent
Wide to the firmament?
Can you, with the simple stature
Of a child, breathing nature,
Become, notwithstanding,
A man?
Can you continue befriending
With no prejudice, no ban?
Can you, mating with heaven,
Serve as the female part?
Can your learned head take leaven
From the wisdom of your heart?
If you can bear issue and nourish its growing,
If you can guide without claim or strife,
If you can stay in the lead of men without their
    knowing,
You are at the core of life.

II

Thirty spokes are made one by holes in a hub
By vacancies joining them for a wheel's use;
The use of clay in moulding pitchers
Comes from the hollow of its absence;
Doors, windows, in a house,
Are used for their emptiness:
Thus we are helped by what is not
To use what is.

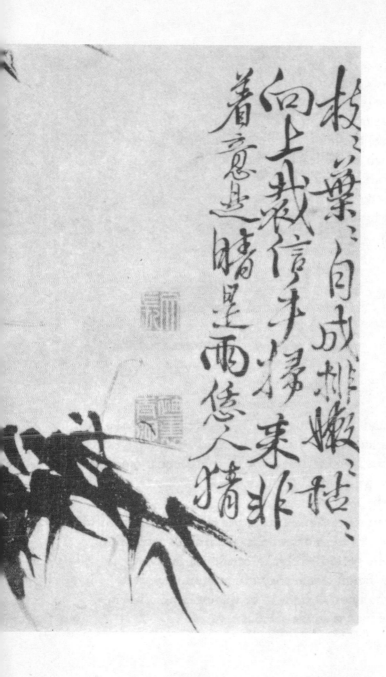

Hsü Wei (1521-1593): Bamboo.

The five colors can blind,
The five tones deafen,
The five tastes cloy.
The race, the hunt, can drive men mad
And their booty leave them no peace.
Therefore a sensible man
Prefers the inner to the outer eye:
He has his yes,—he has his no.

13

Favor and disfavor have been called equal worries,
Success and failure have been called equal ailments.
How can favor and disfavor be called equal worries?
Because winning favor burdens a man
With the fear of losing it.
How can success and failure be called equal ailments?
Because a man thinks of the personal body as self.
When he no longer thinks of the personal body as self
Neither failure nor success can ail him.
One who knows his lot to be the lot of all other men
Is a safe man to guide them,

One who recognizes all men as members of his own
      body
Is a sound man to guard them.

14

What we look for beyond seeing
And call the unseen,
Listen for beyond hearing
And call the unheard,
Grasp for beyond reaching
And call the withheld,
Merge beyond understanding
In a oneness
Which does not merely rise and give light,
Does not merely set and leave darkness,
But forever sends forth a succession of living things as
      mysterious
As the unbegotten existence to which they return.
That is why men have called them empty phenomena,
Meaningless images,
In a mirage
With no face to meet,
No back to follow.
Yet one who is anciently aware of existence
Is master of every moment,
Feels no break since time beyond time
In the way life flows.

明

敏

15

Long ago the land was ruled with a wisdom
Too fine, too deep, to be fully understood
And, since it was beyond men's full understanding,
Only some of it has come down to us, as in these
       sayings:
'Alert as a winter-farer on an icy stream,'
'Wary as a man in ambush,'
'Considerate as a welcome guest,'
'Selfless as melting ice,'
'Green as an uncut tree,'
'Open as a valley,'
And this one also, 'Roiled as a torrent.'
Why roiled as a torrent?
Because when a man is in turmoil how shall he find
      peace
Save by staying patient till the stream clears?
How can a man's life keep its course
If he will not let it flow?
Those who flow as life flows know
They need no other force:
They feel no wear, they feel no tear,
They need no mending, no repair.

16

Be utterly humble
And you shall hold to the foundation of peace.
Be at one with all these living things which, having
  arisen and flourished,
Return to the quiet whence they came,
Like a healthy growth of vegetation
Falling back upon the root.
Acceptance of this return to the root has been called
  'quietism,'
Acceptance of quietism has been condemned as
  'fatalism.'
But fatalism is acceptance of destiny
And to accept destiny is to face life with open eyes,
Whereas not to accept destiny is to face death blindfold.
He who is open-eyed is open-minded,
He who is open-minded is open-hearted,
He who is open-hearted is kingly,
He who is kingly is godly,
He who is godly is useful,
He who is useful is infinite,
He who is infinite is immune,
He who is immune is immortal.

17

A leader is best
When people barely know that he exists,
Not so good when people obey and acclaim him,
Worst when they despise him.
'Fail to honor people,
They fail to honor you;'
But of a good leader, who talks little,
When his work is done, his aim fulfilled,
They will all say, 'We did this ourselves.'

領
袖

18

When people lost sight of the way to live
Came codes of love and honesty,
Learning came, charity came,
Hypocrisy took charge;
When differences weakened family ties
Came benevolent fathers and dutiful sons;
And when lands were disrupted and misgoverned
Came ministers commended as loyal.

損
失

19

Rid of formalized wisdom and learning
People would be a hundredfold happier,
Rid of conventionalized duty and honor
People would find their families dear,
Rid of legalized profiteering
People would have no thieves to fear.
These methods of life have failed, all three,
Here is the way, it seems to me:
Set people free,
As deep in their hearts they would like to be,
From private greeds
And wanton needs.

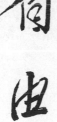

20

Leave off fine learning! End the nuisance
Of saying yes to this and perhaps to that,
Distinctions with how little difference!
Categorical this, categorical that,
What slightest use are they!
If one man leads, another must follow,
How silly that is and how false!
Yet conventional men lead an easy life
With all their days feast-days,
A constant spring visit to the Tall Tower,
While I am a simpleton, a do-nothing,
Not big enough yet to raise a hand,
Not grown enough to smile,
A homeless, worthless waif.
Men of the world have a surplus of goods,
While I am left out, owning nothing.
What a booby I must be
Not to know my way round,
What a fool!
The average man is so crisp and so confident
That I ought to be miserable
Going on and on like the sea,
Drifting nowhere.
All these people are making their mark in the world,
While I, pig-headed, awkward,
Different from the rest,
Am only a glorious infant still nursing at the breast.

21

The surest test if a man be sane
Is if he accepts life whole, as it is,
Without needing by measure or touch to understand
The measureless untouchable source
Of its images,
The measureless untouchable source
Of its substances,
The source which, while it appears dark emptiness,
Brims with a quick force
Farthest away
And yet nearest at hand
From oldest time unto this day,
Charging its images with origin:
What more need I know of the origin
Than this?

'Yield and you need not break:'
Bent you can straighten,
Emptied you can hold,
Torn you can mend;
And as want can reward you
So wealth can bewilder.
Aware of this, a wise man has the simple return
Which other men seek:
Without inflaming himself
He is kindled,
Without explaining himself
Is explained,
Without taking credit
Is accredited,
Laying no claim
Is acclaimed
And, because he does not compete,
Finds peaceful competence.
How true is the old saying,
'Yield and you need not break'!
How completely it comes home!

23

Nature does not have to insist,
Can blow for only half a morning,
Rain for only half a day,
And what are these winds and these rains but natural?
If nature does not have to insist,
Why should man?
It is natural too
That whoever follows the way of life feels alive,
That whoever uses it properly feels well used,
Whereas he who loses the way of life feels lost,
That whoever keeps to the way of life
Feels at home,
Whoever uses it properly
Feels welcome,
Whereas he who uses it improperly
Feels improperly used:
'Fail to honor people,
They fail to honor you.'

24

Standing tiptoe a man loses balance,
Walking astride he has no pace,
Kindling himself he fails to light,
Acquitting himself he forfeits his hearers,
Admiring himself he does so alone.
Pride has never brought a man greatness
But, according to the way of life,
Brings the ills that make him unfit,
Make him unclean in the eyes of his neighbor,
And a sane man will have none of them.

Chang Seng-yu?, early sixth century: The Planet Saturn, from
The Five Planets and Twenty-eight Constellations.

25

Before creation a presence existed,
Self-contained, complete,
Formless, voiceless, mateless,
Changeless,
Which yet pervaded itself
With unending motherhood.
Though there can be no name for it,
I have called it 'the way of life.'
Perhaps I should have called it 'the fullness of life,'
Since fullness implies widening into space,
Implies still further widening,
Implies widening until the circle is whole.
In this sense
The way of life is fulfilled,
Heaven is fulfilled,
Earth fulfilled
And a fit man also is fulfilled:
These are the four amplitudes of the universe
And a fit man is one of them:
Man rounding the way of earth,
Earth rounding the way of heaven,
Heaven rounding the way of life
Till the circle is full.

26

Gravity is the root of grace,
The mainstay of all speed.
A traveler of true means, whatever the day's pace,
Remembers the provision-van
And, however fine prospect be offered, is a man
With a calm head.
What lord of countless chariots would ride them in vain,
Would make himself fool of the realm,
With pace beyond rein,
Speed beyond helm?

27

One may move so well that a foot-print never shows,
Speak so well that the tongue never slips,
Reckon so well that no counter is needed,
Seal an entrance so tight, though using no lock,
That it cannot be opened,
Bind a hold so firm, though using no cord,
That it cannot be untied.
And these are traits not only of a sound man
But of many a man thought to be unsound.

A sound man is good at salvage,
At seeing that nothing is lost.
Having what is called insight,
A good man, before he can help a bad man,
Finds in himself the matter with the bad man.
And whichever teacher
Discounts the lesson
Is as far off the road as the other,
Whatever else he may know.
That is the heart of it.

28

'One who has a man's wings
And a woman's also
Is in himself a womb of the world'
And, being a womb of the world,
Continuously, endlessly,
Gives birth;
One who, preferring light,
Prefers darkness also
Is in himself an image of the world
And, being an image of the world,
Is continuously, endlessly
The dwelling of creation;
One who is highest of men
And humblest also
Is in himself a valley of the world,

And, being a valley of the world,
Continuously, endlessly
Conducts the one source
From which vessels may be usefully filled;
Servants of the state are such vessels,
To be filled from undiminishing supply.

29

Those who would take over the earth
And shape it to their will
Never, I notice, succeed.
The earth is like a vessel so sacred
That at the mere approach of the profane
It is marred
And when they reach out their fingers it is gone.
For a time in the world some force themselves ahead
And some are left behind,
For a time in the world some make a great noise
And some are held silent,
For a time in the world some are puffed fat
And some are kept hungry,
For a time in the world some push aboard
And some are tipped out:
At no time in the world will a man who is sane
Over-reach himself,
Over-spend himself,
Over-rate himself.

30

One who would guide a leader of men in the uses o
Will warn him against the use of arms for conquest.
Weapons often turn upon the wielder,
An army's harvest is a waste of thorns,
Conscription of a multitude of men
Drains the next year dry.
A good general, daring to march, dares also to halt,
Will never press his triumph beyond need.
What he must do he does but not for glory,
What he must do he does but not for show,
What he must do he does but not for self;
He has done it because it had to be done,
Not from a hot head.
Let life ripen and then fall,
Force is not the way at all:
Deny the way of life and you are dead.

f life

instrument of evil,
A spread of plague,
And the way for a vital man to go is not the way of a
    soldier.
But in time of war men civilized in peace
Turn from their higher to their lower nature.
Arms are an instrument of evil,
No measure for thoughtful men
Until there fail all other choice
But sad acceptance of it.
Triumph is not beautiful.
He who thinks triumph beautiful
Is one with a will to kill,
And one with a will to kill
Shall never prevail upon the world.
It is a good sign when man's higher nature comes
    forward,
A bad sign when his lower nature comes forward,
When retainers take charge
And the master stays back
As in the conduct of a funeral.
The death of a multitude is cause for mourning:
Conduct your triumph as a funeral.

32

Existence is infinite, not to be defined;
And, though it seem but a bit of wood in your hand,
      to carve as you please,
It is not to be lightly played with and laid down.
When rulers adhered to the way of life,
They were upheld by natural loyalty:
Heaven and earth were joined and made fertile,
Life was a freshness of rain,
Subject to none,
Free to all.
But men of culture came, with their grades and their
      distinctions;
And as soon as such differences had been devised
No one knew where to end them,
Though the one who does know the end of all such
      differences
Is the sound man:
Existence
Might be likened to the course
Of many rivers reaching the one sea.

33

Knowledge studies others,
Wisdom is self-known;
Muscle masters brothers,
Self-mastery is bone;
Content need never borrow,
Ambition wanders blind:
Vitality cleaves to the marrow
Leaving death behind.

34

Bountiful life, letting anyone attend,
Making no distinction between left or right,
Feeding everyone, refusing no one,
Has not provided this bounty to show how much it
    owns,
Has not fed and clad its guests with any thought of
    claim;
And, because it lacks the twist
Of mind or body in what it has done,
The guile of head or hands,
Is not always respected by a guest.
Others appreciate welcome from the perfect host
Who, barely appearing to exist,
Exists the most.

35

If the sign of life is in your face
He who responds to it
Will feel secure and fit
As when, in a friendly place,
Sure of hearty care,
A traveler gladly waits.
Though it may not taste like food
And he may not see the fare
Or hear a sound of plates,
How endless it is and how good!

36

He who feels punctured
Must once have been a bubble,
He who feels unarmed
Must have carried arms,
He who feels belittled
Must have been consequential,
He who feels deprived
Must have had privilege,
Whereas a man with insight
Knows that to keep under is to endure.
What happens to a fish pulled out of a pond?
Or to an implement of state pulled out of a scabbard?
Unseen, they survive.

37

The way to use life is to do nothing through acting,
The way to use life is to do everything through being.
When a leader knows this,
His land naturally goes straight.
And the world's passion to stray from straightness
Is checked at the core
By the simple unnamable cleanness
Through which men cease from coveting,
And to a land where men cease from coveting
Peace comes of course.

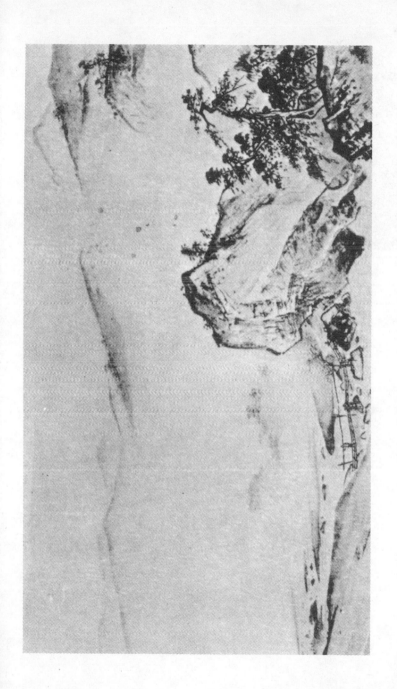

Hsia Kuei (fl. c. 1190-1230): A Pure and Remote View of Rivers and Mountains.

38

A man of sure fitness, without making a point of his
  fitness,
Stays fit;
A man of unsure fitness, assuming an appearance of
  fitness,
Becomes unfit.
The man of sure fitness never makes an act of it
Nor considers what it may profit him;
The man of unsure fitness makes an act of it
And considers what it may profit him.
However a man with a kind heart proceed,
He forgets what it may profit him;
However a man with a just mind proceed,
He remembers what it may profit him;
However a man of conventional conduct proceed, if he
  be not complied with
Out goes his fist to enforce compliance.
Here is what happens:
Losing the way of life, men rely first on their fitness;
Losing fitness, they turn to kindness;
Losing kindness, they turn to justness;
Losing justness, they turn to convention.

Conventions are fealty and honesty gone to waste,
They are the entrance of disorder.
False teachers of life use flowery words
And start nonsense.
The man of stamina stays with the root
Below the tapering,
Stays with the fruit
Beyond the flowering:
He has his no and he has his yes.

39

The wholeness of life has, from of old, been made mani-
      fest in its parts:
Clarity has been made manifest in heaven,
Firmness in earth,
Purity in the spirit,
In the valley conception,
In the river procreation;
And so in a leader are the people made manifest
For wholeness of use.
But for clarity heaven would be veiled,
But for firmness earth would have crumbled,
But for purity spirit would have fumbled,
But for conception the valley would have failed,
But for procreation the river have run dry;
So, save for the people, a leader shall die:
Always the low carry the high
On a root for growing by.
What can stand lofty with no low foundation?
No wonder leaders of a land profess
Their stature and their station
To be servitude and lowliness!
If rim and spoke and hub were not,

Where would be the chariot?
Who will prefer the jingle of jade pendants if
He once has heard stone growing in a cliff!

40

Life on its way returns into a mist,
Its quickness is its quietness again:
Existence of this world of things and men
Renews their never needing to exist.

41

Men of stamina, knowing the way of life,
Steadily keep to it;
Unstable men, knowing the way of life,
Keep to it or not according to occasion;
Stupid men, knowing the way of life
And having once laughed at it, laugh again the louder.
If you need to be sure which way is right, you can tell
       by their laughing at it.
They fling the old charges:
'A wick without oil,'
'For every step forward a step or two back.'
To such laughers a level road looks steep,
Top seems bottom,
'White appears black,'
'Enough is a lack,'
Endurance is a weakness,
Simplicity a faded flower.
But eternity is his who goes straight round the circle,
Foundation is his who can feel beyond touch,
Harmony is his who can hear beyond sound,
Pattern is his who can see beyond shape:
Life is his who can tell beyond words
Fulfillment of the unfulfilled.

42

Life, when it came to be,
Bore one, then two, then three
Elements of things;
And thus the three began
—Heaven and earth and man—
To balance happenings:
Cool night behind, warm day ahead,
For the living, for the dead.
Though a commoner be loth to say
That he is only common clay,
Kings and princes often state
How humbly they are leading,
Because in true succeeding
High and low correlate.
It is an ancient thought,

Which many men have taught,
That he who over-reaches
And tries to live by force
Shall die thereby of course,
And is what my own heart teaches.

43

As the soft yield of water cleaves obstinate stone,
So to yield with life solves the insoluble:
To yield, I have learned, is to come back again.
But this unworded lesson,
This easy example,
Is lost upon men.

44

Which means more to you,
You or your renown?
Which brings more to you,
You or what you own?
And which would cost you more
If it were gone?
The niggard pays,
The miser loses.
The least ashamed of men
Goes back if he chooses:
He knows both ways,
He starts again.

45

A man's work, however finished it seem,
Continues as long as he live;
A man, however perfect he seem,
Is needed as long as he live:
As long as truth appears falsity,
The seer a fool,
The prophet a dumb lout,
If you want to keep warm keep stirring about,
Keep still if you want to keep cool,
And in all the world one day no doubt
Your way shall be the rule.

46

In a land where the way of life is understood
Race-horses are led back to serve the field;
In a land where the way of life is not understood
War-horses are bred on the autumn yield.
Owning is the entanglement,
Wanting is the bewilderment,
Taking is the presentiment:
Only he who contains content
Remains content.

47

There is no need to run outside
For better seeing,
Nor to peer from a window. Rather abide
At the center of your being;
For the more you leave it, the less you learn.
Search your heart and see
If he is wise who takes each turn:
The way to do is to be.

48

A man anxious for knowledge adds more to himself
    every minute;
A man acquiring life loses himself in it,
Has less and less to bear in mind,
Less and less to do,
Because life, he finds, is well inclined,
Including himself too.
Often a man sways the world like a wind
But not by deed;
And if there appear to you to be need
Of motion to sway it, it has left you behind.

49

A sound man's heart is not shut within itself
But is open to other people's hearts:
I find good people good,
And I find bad people good
If I am good enough;
I trust men of their word,
And I trust liars
If I am true enough;
I feel the heart-beats of others
Above my own
If I am enough of a father,
Enough of a son.

50

Death might appear to be the issue of life,
Since for every three out of ten being born
Three out of ten are dying.
Then why
Should another three out of ten continue breeding
    death?
Because of sheer madness to multiply.
But there is one out of ten, they say, so sure of life
That tiger and wild bull keep clear of his inland path,
Weapons turn from him on the battle-field.
No bull-horn could tell where to gore him,
No tiger-claw where to tear him,
No weapon where to enter him.
And why?
Because he has no death to die.

使

愛

51

Existence having born them
And fitness bred them,
While matter varied their forms
And breath empowered them,
All created things render, to the existence and fitness
        they depend on,
An obedience
Not commanded but of course.
And since this is the way existence bears issue
And fitness raises, attends,
Shelters, feeds and protects,
Do you likewise:
Be parent, not possessor,
Attendant, not master,
Be concerned not with obedience but with benefit,
And you are at the core of living.

5²

The source of life
Is as a mother.
Be fond of both mother and children but know the
      mother dearer
And you outlive death.
Curb your tongue and senses
And you are beyond trouble,
Let them loose
And you are beyond help.
Discover that nothing is too small for clear vision,
Too insignificant for tender strength,
Use outlook
And insight,
Use them both
And you are immune:
For you have witnessed eternity.

53

If I had any learning
Of a highway wide and fit,
Would I lose it at each turning?
Yet look at people spurning
Natural use of it!
See how fine the palaces
And see how poor the farms,
How bare the peasants' granaries
While gentry wear embroideries
Hiding sharpened arms,
And the more they have the more they seize,
How can there be such men as these
Who never hunger, never thirst,
Yet eat and drink until they burst!
There are other brigands, but these are the worst
Of all the highway's harms.

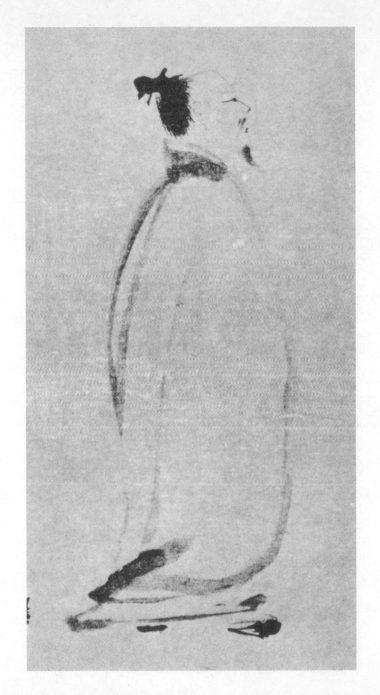

Liang K'ai (fl. mid-thirteenth century): Li Po Chanting a Poem.

54

'Since true foundation cannot fail
But holds as good as new,
Many a worshipful son shall hail
A father who lived true.'
Realized in one man, fitness has its rise;
Realized in a family, fitness multiplies;
Realized in a village, fitness gathers weight;
Realized in a country, fitness becomes great;
Realized in the world, fitness fills the skies.
And thus the fitness of one man
You find in the family he began,
You find in the village that accrued,
You find in the country that ensued,
You find in the world's whole multitude.
How do I know this integrity?
Because it could all begin in me.

55

He whom life fulfills,
Though he remains a child,
Is immune to the poisonous sting
Of insects, to the ravening
Of wild beasts or to vultures' bills.
He needs no more bone or muscle than a baby's for
      sure hold.
Without thought of joined organs, he is gender
Which grows firm, unfaltering.
Though his voice should cry out at full pitch all day,
      it would not rasp but would stay tender
Through the perfect balancing
Of a man at endless ease with everything
Because of the true life that he has led.
To try for more than this bodes ill.
It is said, 'there's a way where there's a will;'
But let life ripen and then fall.
Will is not the way at all:
Deny the way of life and you are dead.

56

Those who know do not tell,
Those who tell do not know.
Not to set the tongue loose
But to curb it,
Not to have edges that catch
But to remain untangled,
Unblinded,
Unconfused,
Is to find balance,
And he who holds balance beyond sway of love or hate,
Beyond reach of profit or loss,
Beyond care of praise or blame,
Has attained the highest post in the world.

57

A realm is governed by ordinary acts,
A battle is governed by extraordinary acts;
The world is governed by no acts at all.
And how do I know?
This is how I know.
Act after act prohibits
Everything but poverty,
Weapon after weapon conquers
Everything but chaos,
Business after business provides
A craze of waste,
Law after law breeds
A multitude of thieves.
Therefore a sensible man says:
If I keep from meddling with people, they take care of
     themselves,
If I keep from commanding people, they behave them-
     selves,
If I keep from preaching at people, they improve
     themselves,
If I keep from imposing on people, they become
     themselves.

領袖

58

The less a leader does and says
The happier his people,
The more a leader struts and brags
The sorrier his people.
Often what appears to be unhappiness is happiness
And what appears to be happiness is unhappiness.
Who can see what leads to what
When happiness appears and yet is not,
When what should be is nothing but a mask
Disguising what should not be? Who can but ask
An end to such a stupid plot!
Therefore a sound man shall so square the circle
And circle the square as not to injure, not to impede:
The glow of his life shall not daze,
It shall lead.

59

To lead men and serve heaven, weigh the worth
Of the one source:
Use the single force
Which doubles the strength of the strong
By enabling man to go right, disabling him to go
  wrong,
Be so charged with the nature of life that you give your
  people birth,
That you mother your land, are the fit
And ever-living root of it:
The seeing·root, whose eye is infinite.

60

Handle a large kingdom with as gentle a touch as if
  you were cooking small fish.
If you manage people by letting them alone,
Ghosts of the dead shall not haunt you.
Not that there are no ghosts
But that their influence becomes propitious
In the sound existence of a living man:
There is no difference between the quick and the dead,
They are one channel of vitality.

61

A large country is the low level of interflowing rivers.
It draws people to the sea-end of a valley
As the female draws the male,
Receives it into absorbing depth
Because depth always absorbs.
And so a large country, inasfar as it is deeper than a
      small country,
Absorbs the small—
Or a small country, inasfar as it is deeper than a large
      country,
Absorbs the large.
Some countries consciously seek depth into which to
      draw others.
Some countries naturally have depth into which to draw
      others:
A large country needs to admit,
A small country needs to emit,
And so each country can naturally have what it needs
If the large country submit.

62

Existence is sanctuary:
It is a good man's purse,
It is also a bad man's keep.
Clever performances come dear or cheap,
Goodness comes free;
And how shall a man who acts better deny a man who
       acts worse
This right to be.
Rather, when an emperor is crowned, let the three
Ministers whom he appoints to receive for him fine
       horses and gifts of jade
Receive for him also the motionless gift of integrity,
The gift prized as highest by those ancients who said,
'Only pursue an offender to show him the way.'
What men in all the world could have more wealth than
       they?

63

Men knowing the way of life
Do without acting,
Effect without enforcing,
Taste without consuming;
'Through the many they find the few,
Through the humble the great;'
They 'respect their foes,'
They 'face the simple fact before it becomes involved.
Solve the small problem before it becomes big.'
The most involved fact in the world
Could have been faced when it was simple,
The biggest problem in the world
Could have been solved when it was small.
The simple fact that he finds no problem big
Is a sane man's prime achievement.
If you say yes too quickly
You may have to say no,
If you think things are done too easily
You may find them hard to do:
If you face trouble sanely
It cannot trouble you.

64

Before it move, hold it,
Before it go wrong, mould it,
Drain off water in winter before it freeze,
Before weeds grow, sow them to the breeze.
You can deal with what has not happened, can foresee
Harmful events and not allow them to be.
Though—as naturally as a seed becomes a tree of arm-
    wide girth—
There can rise a nine-tiered tower from a man's handful
    of earth
Or here at your feet a thousand-mile journey have birth,
Quick action bruises,
Quick grasping loses.
Therefore a sane man's care is not to exert
One move that can miss, one move that can hurt.
Most people who miss, after almost winning,
Should have 'known the end from the beginning.'
A sane man is sane in knowing what things he can
    spare,
In not wishing what most people wish,
In not reaching for things that seem rare.
The cultured might call him heathenish,
This man of few words, because his one care
Is not to interfere but to let nature renew
The sense of direction men undo.

Ni Tsan (1301-1374): Trees in a River Valley at Yü-shan
(1371).

65

Sound old rulers, it is said,
Left people to themselves, instead
Of wanting to teach everything
And start the people arguing.
With mere instruction in command,
So that people understand
Less than they know, woe is the land;
But happy the land that is ordered so
That they understand more than they know.
For everyone's good this double key
Locks and unlocks equally.
If modern man would use it, he
Could find old wisdom in his heart
And clear his vision enough to see
From start to finish and finish to start
The circle rounding perfectly.

66

Why are rivers and seas lords of the waters?
Because they afford the common level
And so become lords of the waters.
The common people love a sound man
Because he does not talk above their level,
Because, though he lead them,
He follows them,
He imposes no weight on them;
And they in turn, because he does not impede them,
Yield to him, content:
People never tire of anyone
Who is not bent upon comparison.

67

Everyone says that my way of life is the way of a
    simpleton.
Being largely the way of a simpleton is what makes it
    worth while.
If it were not the way of a simpleton
It would long ago have been worthless,
These possessions of a simpleton being the three I
    choose
And cherish:
To care,
To be fair,
To be humble.
When a man cares he is unafraid,
When he is fair he leaves enough for others,
When he is humble he can grow;
Whereas if, like men of today, he be bold without
    caring,
Self-indulgent without sharing,
Self-important without shame,
He is dead.
The invincible shield
Of caring
Is a weapon from the sky
Against being dead.

68

The best captain does not plunge headlong
Nor is the best soldier a fellow hot to fight.
The greatest victor wins without a battle:
He who overcomes men understands them.
There is a quality of quietness
Which quickens people by no stress:
'Fellowship with heaven,' as of old,
Is fellowship with man and keeps its hold.

69

The handbook of the strategist has said:
'Do not invite the fight, accept it instead,'
'Better a foot behind than an inch too far ahead,'
Which means:
Look a man straight in the face and make no move,
Roll up your sleeve and clench no fist,
Open your hand and show no weapon,
Bare your breast and find no foe.
But as long as there be a foe, value him,
Respect him, measure him, be humble toward him;
Let him not strip from you, however strong he be,
Compassion, the one wealth which can afford him.

70

My way is so simple to feel, so easy to apply,
That only a few will feel it or apply it.
If it were not the lasting way, the natural way to try,
If it were a passing way, everyone would try it.
But however few shall go my way
Or feel concerned with me,
Some there are and those are they
Who witness what they see:
Sanity is a haircloth sheath
With a jewel underneath.

71

A man who knows how little he knows is well,
A man who knows how much he knows is sick.
If, when you see the symptoms, you can tell,
Your cure is quick.
A sound man knows that sickness makes him sick
And before he catches it his cure is quick.

72

Upon those who defy authority
It shall be visited,
But not behind prison walls
Nor through oppression of their kin;
Men sanely led
Are not led by duress.
To know yourself and not show yourself,
To think well of yourself and not tell of yourself,
Be that your no and your yes.

73

A man with outward courage dares to die,
A man with inward courage dares to live;
But either of these men
Has a better and a worse side than the other.
And who can tell exactly to which qualities heaven
        objects?
Heaven does nothing to win the day,
Says nothing—
Is echoed,
Orders nothing—
Is obeyed,
Advises nothing—
Is right:
And which of us, seeing that nothing is outside the vast
Wide-meshed net of heaven, knows just how it is cast?

74

Death is no threat to people
Who are not afraid to die;
But even if these offenders feared death all day,
Who should be rash enough
To act as executioner?
Nature is executioner.
When man usurps the place,
A carpenter's apprentice takes the place of the master:
And 'an apprentice hacking with the master's axe
May slice his own hand.'

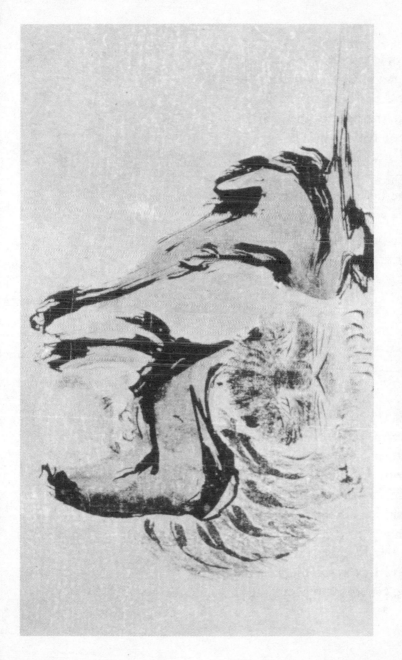

Anonymous, thirteenth century?: Patriarch and Tiger. From a pair of scrolls representing Two Patriarchs Harmonizing their Minds.

75

People starve
If taxes eat their grain,
And the faults of starving people
Are the fault of their rulers.
That is why people rebel.
Men who have to fight for their living
And are not afraid to die for it
Are higher men than those who, stationed high,
Are too fat to dare to die.

76

Man, born tender and yielding,
Stiffens and hardens in death.
All living growth is pliant,
Until death transfixes it.
Thus men who have hardened are 'kin of death'
And men who stay gentle are 'kin of life.'
Thus a hard-hearted army is doomed to lose.
A tree hard-fleshed is cut down:
Down goes the tough and big,
Up comes the tender sprig.

77

生
存

Is not existence
Like a drawn bow?
The ends approach,
The height shortens, the narrowness widens.
True living would take from those with too much
Enough for those with too little,
Whereas man exacts from those with too little
Still more for those with too much.
Now what man shall have wealth enough to share with
       all men
Save one who can freely draw from the common means?
A sane man needs no better support, no richer reward,
Than this common means,
Through which he is all men's equal.

78

What is more fluid, more yielding than water?
Yet back it comes again, wearing down the rigid
    strength
Which cannot yield to withstand it.
So it is that the strong are overcome by the weak,
The haughty by the humble.
This we know
But never learn,
So that when wise men tell us,
'He who bites the dust
Is owner of the earth,
He who is scapegoat
Is king,'
They seem to twist the truth.

79

If terms to end a quarrel leave bad feeling,
What good are they?
So a sensible man takes the poor end of the bargain
Without quibbling.
It is sensible to make terms,
Foolish to be a stickler:
Though heaven prefer no man,
A sensible man prefers heaven.

80

If a land is small and its people are few,
With tenfold enough to have and to do,
And if no one has schooled them to waste supply
In the country for which they live and would die,
Then not a boat, not a cart
Tempts this people to depart,
Not a dagger, not a bow
Has to be drawn or bent for show,
People reckon by knots in a cord,
Relish plain food on the board,
Simple clothing suits them well,
And they remain content to dwell
In homes their customs can afford.
Though so close to their own town another town grow
They can hear its dogs bark and its roosters crow,
Yet glad of life in the village they know,
Where else in the world shall they need to go?

81

Real words are not vain,
Vain words not real;
And since those who argue prove nothing
A sensible man does not argue.
A sensible man is wiser than he knows,
While a fool knows more than is wise.
Therefore a sensible man does not devise resources:
The greater his use to others
The greater their use to him,
The more he yields to others
The more they yield to him.
The way of life cleaves without cutting:
Which, without need to say,
Should be man's way.

方
法